Praise for **Forever Frien**

and the *Rainbow Reach Series*

"Susan Weaver has created the *Rainbow Reach Series* as a comprehensive tool for children to express thoughts and feelings involving death and loss. From pet loss, to worry, deployment and death, these interactive workbooks create the safe space for expression so needed for our bereaved girls and boys. Parents and professionals will assuredly benefit from using these resources to develop communication and sharing, and normalize a child's grief journey. The *Rainbow Reach Series* is a valuable tool for young people and adults to use in recognizing the multifaceted aspects of grieving, and for supporting outlooks for recovery and resilience that can be useful throughout a lifetime."

Linda Goldman, Grief Therapist and Educator
Author of: *Life and Loss, Children Also Grieve,* and *Raising Our Children to Be Resilient*

"Children heal best when they are engaged in activities that help them express and resolve difficult feelings. The *Rainbow Reach Series* provides such activities in a creative, interesting workbook format that will help children move beyond grief and anxiety."

Mary W. Lindahl, Ph.D.
Professor of Psychology, Marymount University
Licensed Clinical Psychologist

"The *Rainbow Reach Series* is wonderful! I love the way that a child's creativity is utilized in identifying emotions and focusing on blessings. The books offer excellent yet simple text and drive the lessons of optimism, acceptance of feelings and resilience home in truly age-appropriate ways. Bravo!"

Fran Zamore, MSW, ACSW
Author of: *GriefWork – Healing from Loss* and
The GriefWork Companion – Activities for Healing
Bereavement Coordinator, Holy Cross Hospice – Silver Spring, MD
Private Practice

"As a licensed clinical psychologist, with several years of experience helping children with the issues contained in the *Rainbow Reach Series*, I would utilize the books in a child's therapy to help them learn how to express difficult thoughts and feelings. The books are colorful, engaging, and easy to use, and the activities will help children address the impact of life events in healthy ways."

Lynn J. Piper, Ph.D., LCP
Animal Assisted and Trauma Therapist

(continued)

Praise for **Forever Friend**
and the *Rainbow Reach Series* (continued)

"The key to recovery from significant emotional loss is to express feelings in the moment you have them. Children are naturally superb at communicating what they feel when they feel it. The *Rainbow Reach Series* of books presents perfect guidelines for children to help them discover what they need and want to communicate about life-affecting events, in pictures and words. We heartily endorse these books – and heart is the most important element."

Russell Friedman & John W. James
Co-authors of: *The Grief Recovery Handbook* and *When Children Grieve*
www.grief.net

Praise for other books in the *Rainbow Reach Series*

Worry Busters!

"I particularly like the *Worry Busters!* activity that helps children decide how <u>big</u> their worry is and how to make their worry smaller."

Nancy S. Price, LCSW
Licensed Clinical Social Worker

Heroes!

"Just like their soldier dads and moms, many military children are experiencing an extraordinary number of deployments resulting in disruptions in their home routines and stress. They often feel they must take on additional family responsibilities in the absence of their deployed parent and can become overwhelmed.

AUSA Family Programs is continually searching for beneficial resources to offer military parents to help them address these challenges. I highly recommend Susan Weaver's *Rainbow Reach Series* of books for younger children. These insightful workbooks will address not only sensitive issues such as worry and the deployment of a parent but also the loss of a loved one or even a family pet. Using both pictures and words, they offer a means for a child to be able to communicate his/her emotions and thoughts about life affecting events."

Sylvia E. J. Kidd
Director of Family Programs
Association of the US Army (AUSA)

FOREVER FRIEND

Activities for Kids Who Have Lost a Pet

by Susan B. Weaver

Published by:

www.rainbowreach.com

Rainbow Reach
Post Office Box 461
Herndon, VA 20172-0461 U.S.A.
www.rainbowreach.com

Other books in the *Rainbow Reach Series...*

     Love & Memories: *Activities for Kids Who Have Lost a Loved One*

     Heroes! *Activities for Kids Dealing with Deployment*

     Worry Busters! *Activities for Kids Who Worry Too Much*

Weaver, Susan B.
     Forever Friend: *Activities for Kids Who Have Lost a Pet*
     SUMMARY: A book to help children work through grief associated with the death
          or loss of a pet. Includes drawing and writing activities that enable a child's
          feelings to be expressed.
     Audience: Ages 4-14

Printed in the United States of America on Acid-Free Paper
10 9 8 7 6 5 4 3 2 1

ISBN: 978-0-9829490-4-7
Library of Congress Control Number: 2011920729

1. Children. 2. Grief. 3. Pet Loss.

A Note to Grown-Ups

Our natural reaction to loss and grief, in the lives of those we love, is to help them feel better. It seems as if taking their minds off what has happened will help, but in the long run this can make things worse by suppressing important feelings and emotions. The key to resolving loss and grief is to address the situation, identify feelings, and to move beyond the hurt.

Children are better able to understand what's going on around them when they can talk about what's on their minds rather than remaining silent and burying their feelings. This activity book provides an opportunity to connect with children and young adults so you can help guide them through this difficult time. The activities will allow them to work through feelings they may not understand, to express their thoughts and emotions, and to get answers to questions they may not otherwise ask. Developing these communication skills at a young age will foster a lifetime of solutions for kids, help to build self-esteem, and teach them how to cope with these types of situations in the future.

Young children will need a great deal of assistance completing these activities. They may not understand that their pet is not coming back. Younger children may think their thoughts, behavior, or actions are responsible for the death of their pet, or that they will be able to bring their pet back to life through a change in behavior or by believing in miracles.

Older children will be able to complete the activities on their own, but may still welcome your love and assistance as they fill in the book. By setting an example of how YOU feel, you can show kids that it's ok (and healthy) to express their own emotions. They will always miss their pet, but creating positive memories, and saying goodbye, will allow the healing process to begin.

Color these pages!

Filling these activity pages with color will create a vibrant keepsake for kids. It defines a celebration of their pet's LIFE which they can always use to remember their beloved pet.

There are ALL KINDS of ways you can HONOR and REMEMBER your pet!

In Loving Memory Of Your Pet:

Pet's Name: _____

Today's Date: _____

Let's get started!

Draw a picture of your pet here.

Who else will miss your pet?
Ask them to sign this Guest Page!
Or fill in their names below.

Guests

They can share thoughts and stories...

And help fill in this book!

Ask guests to write thoughts and tell stories about your pet...

Draw your pet running, jumping, flying, resting or playing!

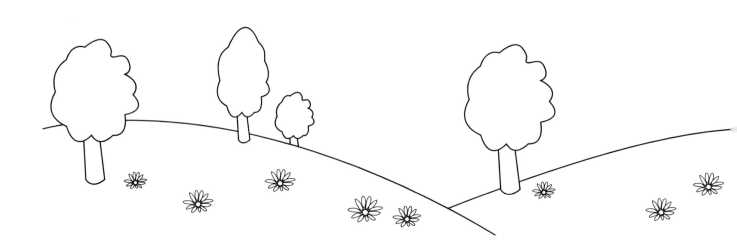

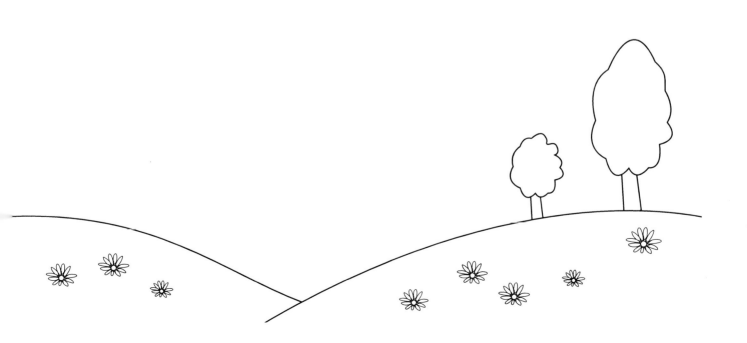

Who can you talk to or who do you WISH you could talk to about questions you might have?

Your Mom

Your Favorite Teacher

Your Grandma

Your Grandpa

Your Stepmom

Your Dad

Your Stepdad

Your Uncle

Your Best Friend's Mom or Dad

Your Aunt

A Trusted Neighbor

Your Brother

Your Sister

Someone else?

Who? _____

Why don't you ask this person your questions and see if he or she will help you fill in this book!

Do you know that whatever happened to your pet...

1 ...it was not your fault...

2 ...you did not cause it to happen...

3 ...there is nothing you or anyone else could have done to prevent it?

Do you have questions about what happened to your pet? Write your questions here:

_____

_____

_____

_____

_____

_____

_____

Families have different beliefs about where pets go when they die.

Ask someone in your family about these beliefs.

Draw pictures of how your pet might look in this place!

Write down the first memory you have of your pet.

Where did you get your pet?

How did your pet get his or her name?

How excited were you?

Who fed and took care of your pet?

Draw a picture of your memory here!

Be sure to include any special spots or markings your pet had!

How do you feel most of the time since your pet is gone?

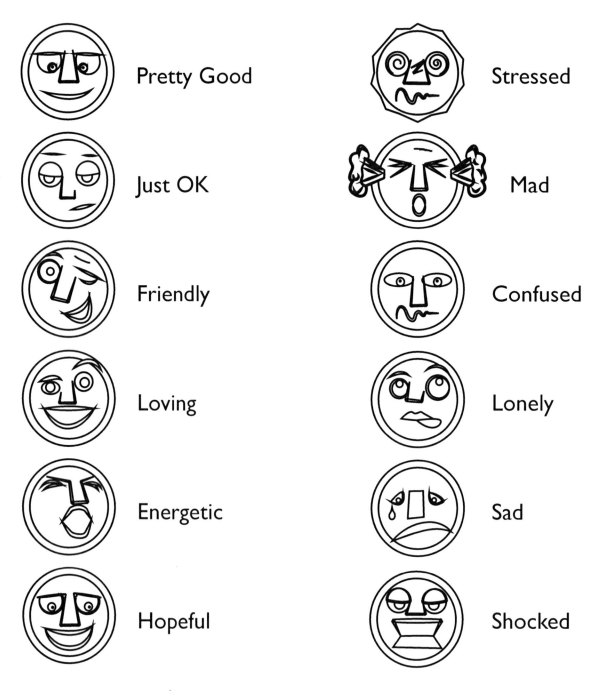

Pretty Good

Just OK

Friendly

Loving

Energetic

Hopeful

Stressed

Mad

Confused

Lonely

Sad

Shocked

My feelings keep changing back and forth all the time.

Draw pictures of how you feel...

For Example:

It's OK to feel sad, mad, lonely...or to switch back and forth.

You may feel very sad one day, mad the next, and happy the next...
or you may feel all of these things in the same day!
It can be very confusing.

It's good to let your feelings out!

It's a good idea to talk with a trusted grown-up about how you feel so you can work through your feelings.

If you feel really mad or upset, here are some things that might help...

Take some deep breaths.

Play sports.

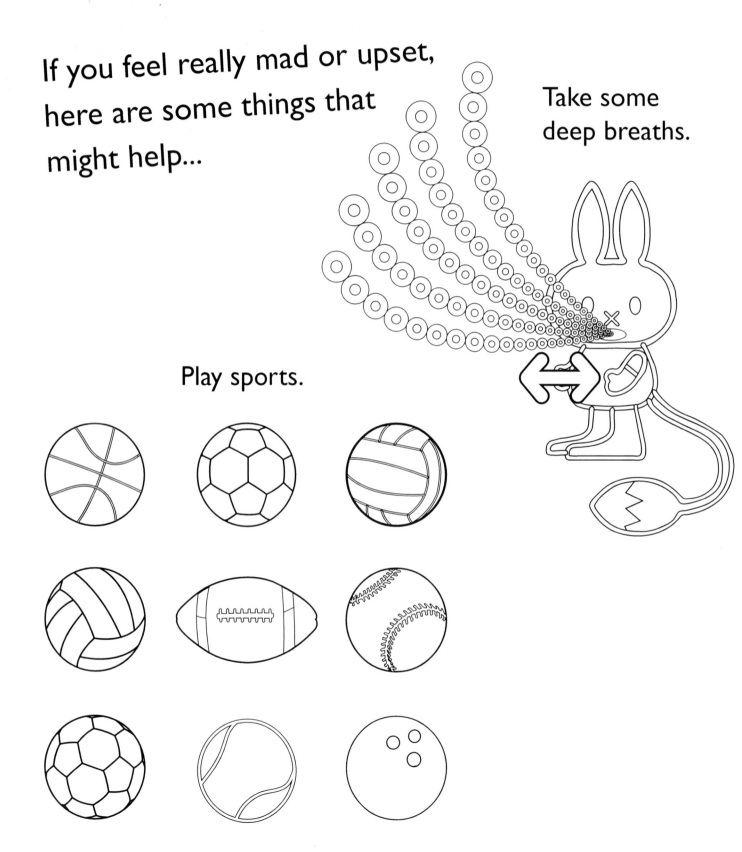

Go outside and
jump up and down
or run around!

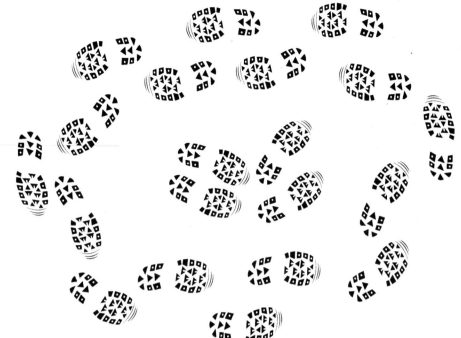

Get some exercise!

Can you think of some things that may make you feel better?

_____   _____

_____   _____

_____   _____

_____   _____

Frame pictures of your pet!

1) Get some pictures of your pet...
   (ask a grown-up what pictures you can use)

2) Place the pictures on these pages...
   (attach the pictures with glue or tape)

3) Color a frame around each picture!

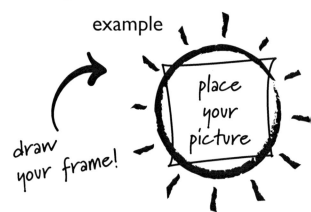

example

draw your frame!

place your picture

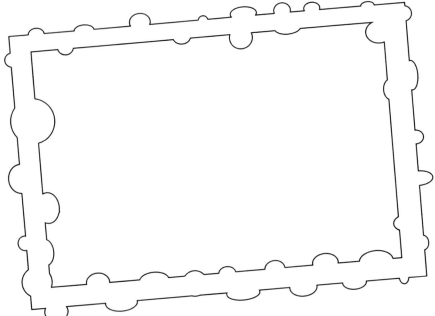

Frame more pictures here!

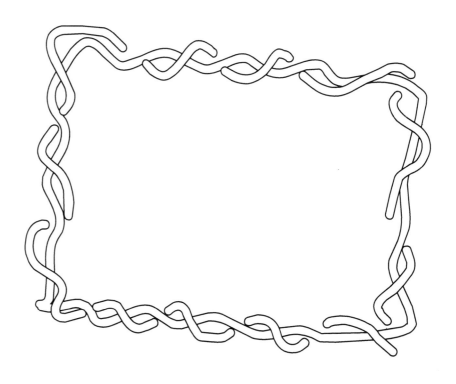

Color your pet's favorite season!

What did your pet like the most about this season?

_____

_____

_____

_____

_____

_____

Draw some of your pet's favorite things.

Which of these things did your pet like?

Sun?

Snow?

Mud?

Rain?

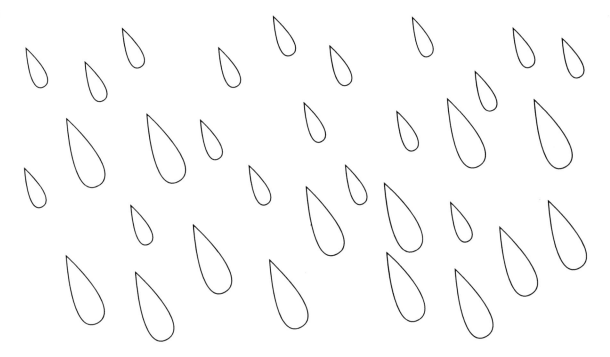

The
Ocean?

What did your pet like the most?

Why did he or she like it?

Draw a picture of what your pet liked the most!

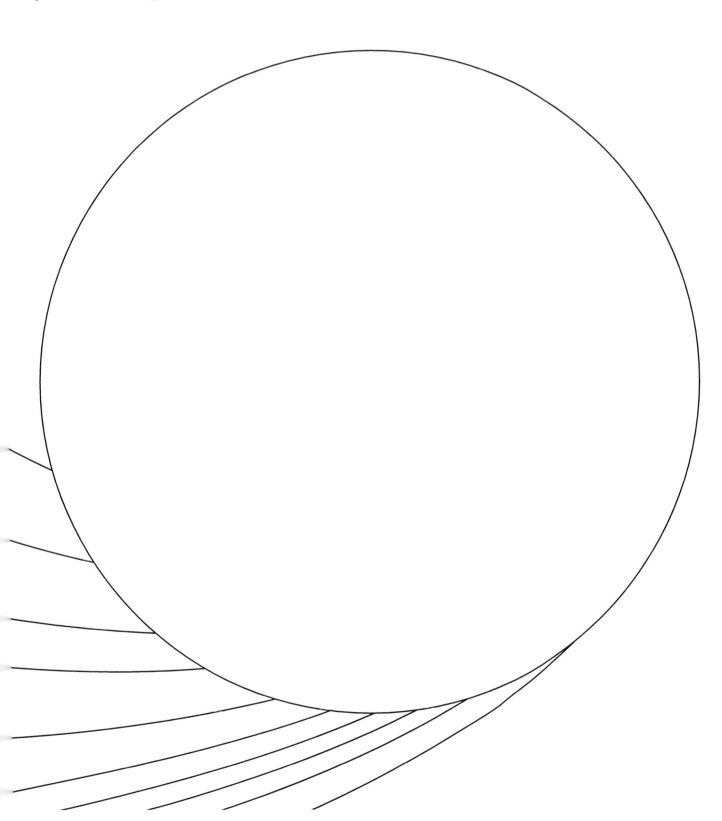

What was it you especially loved about your pet?

Sounds your pet made?

How he or she looked at you?

Kisses?

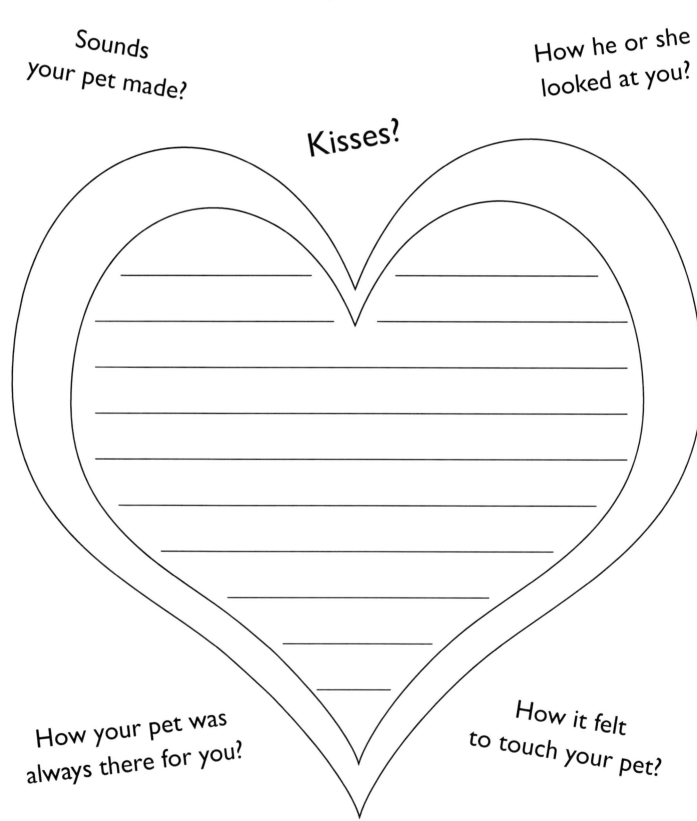

How your pet was always there for you?

How it felt to touch your pet?

Draw this in a picture, or draw how this made you feel.

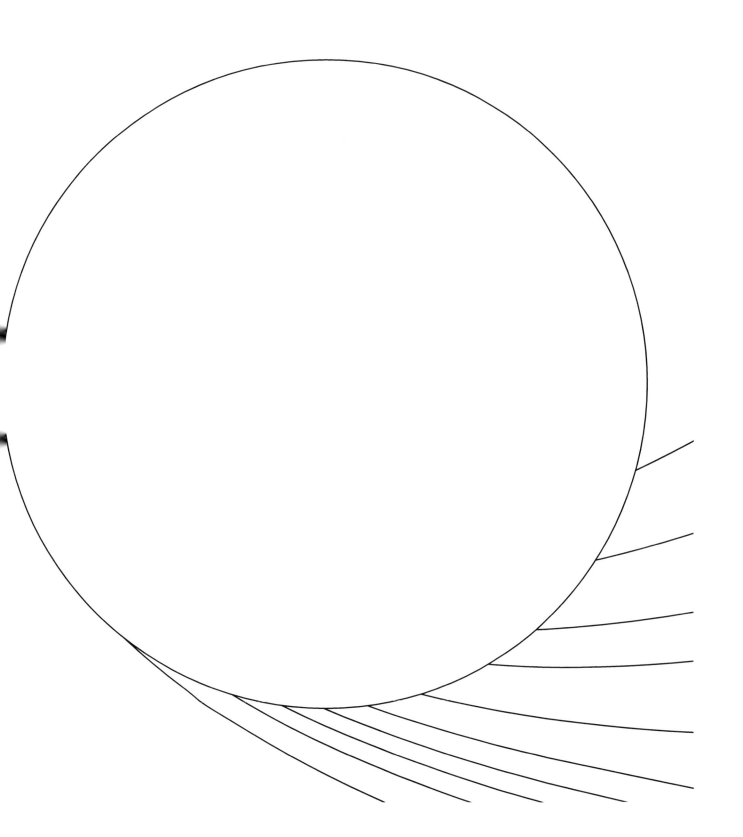

Was there anything you did NOT especially love about your pet?

It's OK if there are things you didn't like or wished had been different.

That doesn't mean you didn't love him or her.

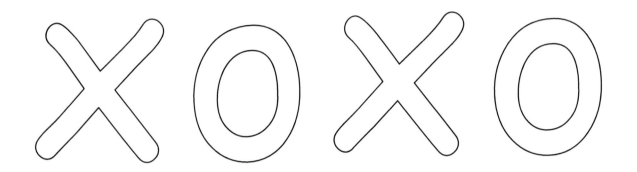

What are some things you wished had been different about your pet?

_____

_____

_____

_____

_____

_____

_____

Did your pet take naps during the day?

Did your pet lie on his or her back?

Where was your pet's favorite place to nap?

_____

write your pet's favorite place to nap here

Draw a picture of your pet napping!

Where did your pet sleep at night?

_____

write it here

Draw a picture of where your pet used to sleep and how comfortable he or she was.

What were your pet's FAVORITE places?

Outside?

_____

_____

_____

_____

_____

Inside?

On your lap?

Draw pictures of your pet in these places!

Did your pet have other animal friends?

What were their names?

Did your pet have a nickname?
What was it? _____

What were your pet's favorite toys?
_____

_____

_____

What were your pet's favorite foods?
_____

_____

_____

What are the smartest things your pet ever did?
_____

_____

_____

_____

_____

How big was your pet?

9 feet tall
108 inches tall

8 feet tall
96 inches tall

7 feet tall
84 inches tall

6 feet tall
72 inches tall

5 feet tall
60 inches tall

4 feet tall
48 inches tall

3 feet tall
36 inches tall

2 feet tall
24 inches tall

1 foot tall
12 inches tall

0 feet tall
1 inch tall

As Big As
A Giraffe?

Giraffes
are
around
19
feet
tall.

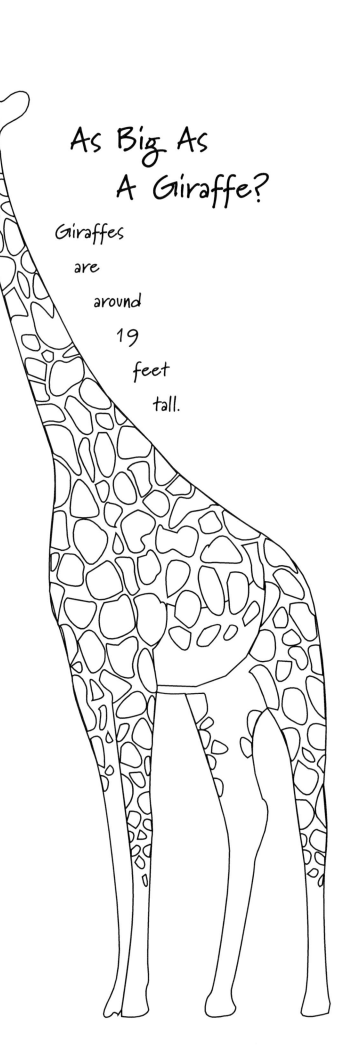

As Small
As A Mouse?

A mouse is about 2 inches tall...
4 inches if standing up!

Did your pet have a schedule?

What did your pet do at different times of the day?

Schedule During the Week

6 am - 9 am   _____

            _____

9 am - 11 am   _____

            _____

11 am - 1 pm   _____

            _____

1 pm - 3 pm   _____

            _____

3 pm - 5 pm   _____

            _____

5 pm - 7 pm   _____

            _____

7 pm - Bedtime _____

            _____

Did you have more time to spend
with your pet on weekends?

Did that make a difference in his or her schedule?

Schedule On Weekends

6 am - 9 am   _____

_____

9 am - 11 am   _____

_____

11 am - 1 pm   _____

_____

pm - 3 pm   _____

_____

3 pm - 5 pm   _____

_____

5 pm - 7 pm   _____

_____

7 pm - Bedtime   _____

_____

How did you spend time with your pet?

Talking?

Taking walks?

Playing?

Hanging out?

List some things you did together...

_____

_____

_____

_____

_____

Draw pictures of things you did!

Are there things you wish you had done differently with your pet while he or she was here?

Write down anything you wish you had done differently with your pet.

_____

_____

_____

_____

_____

_____

_____

_____

_____

_____

_____

_____

If you could see your pet one more time, what would you say to him or her?

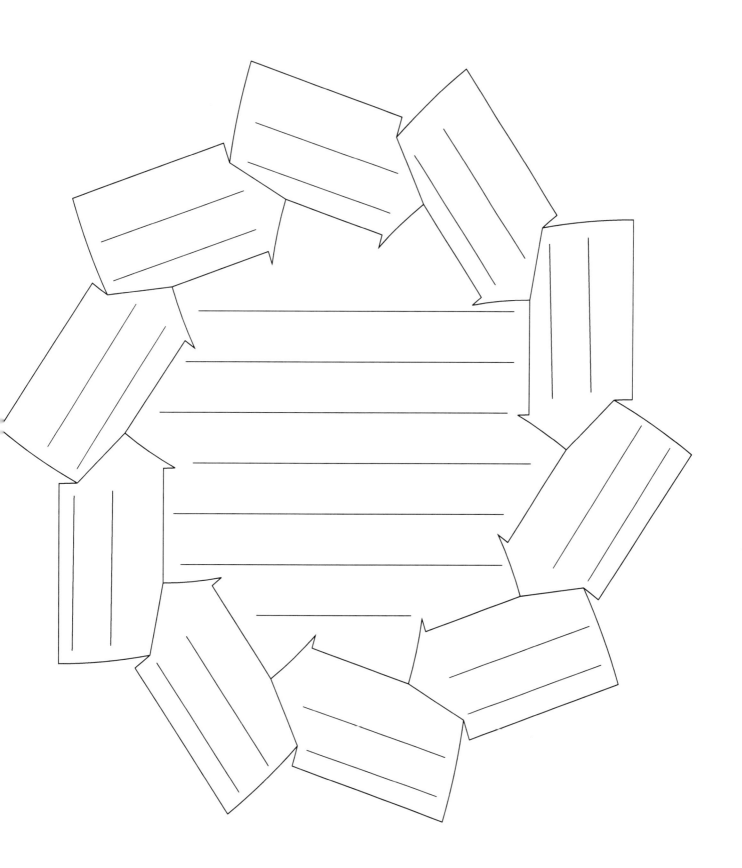

Can you think of ways your pet changed your life for the better?

My pet taught me how to be responsible.

I learned a lot about love from my pet.

My pet gave me confidence!

My pet taught me to always think of others.

Draw some of these positive changes!

Write some words that describe your pet...

_____   _____

_____   _____

_____   _____

_____   _____

_____   _____

_____

Now make up a <u>story</u> or <u>poem</u> about your pet using the words you wrote!

You might want to ask

for help on this one!

Once upon a time...

...even though my pet is not here now, I have lots of great memories.

Write more stories or poems...

_____

_____

_____

_____

_____

_____

_____

_____

_____

_____

_____

_____

_____

_____

_____

What is your favorite song?

Write the name of the song here: _____

Now write down the words as you sing the song.

Here are some suggestions if you cannot think of a song!

ABC
Bingo
Crocodile Rock
Eye Of The Tiger
Fearless
Fireflies
Firework
Hickory Dickory Dock
Hokey Pokey
How To Save A Life
I Gotta Feeling

I'm A Little Teapot
It's A Small World
Itsy Bitsy Spider
Just The Way You Are
Macarena
Mary Had A Little Lamb
Never Say Never
Old McDonald Had A Farm
Paparazzi
Ring Around The Rosie
Row Row Row Your Boat
The Lion Sleeps Tonight
Three Blind Mice

Twinkle Twinkle Little Star
We Are The Champions
We Will Rock You
Yankee Doodle
Yellow Submarine
You Belong With Me

Substitute some words to make this a song about your wonderful pet!

_____

_____

_____

_____

_____

_____

_____

_____

_____

_____

_____

_____

_____

Try this using another song!

Write a letter to your pet!

Tell your pet how much you will always love him or her, and how important he or she will always be to you. Say goodbye to your beloved pet if you can.

_____

_____

_____

_____

_____

_____

_____

_____

_____

_____

_____

_____

Use these pages if you want to write more.

_____

_____

_____

_____

_____

_____

_____

_____

_____

_____

_____

_____

_____

_____

When you're done writing your letter, read it out loud to someone you love.

Write down your MOST wonderful memory of your pet...

What were you doing?

Were you with somebody?

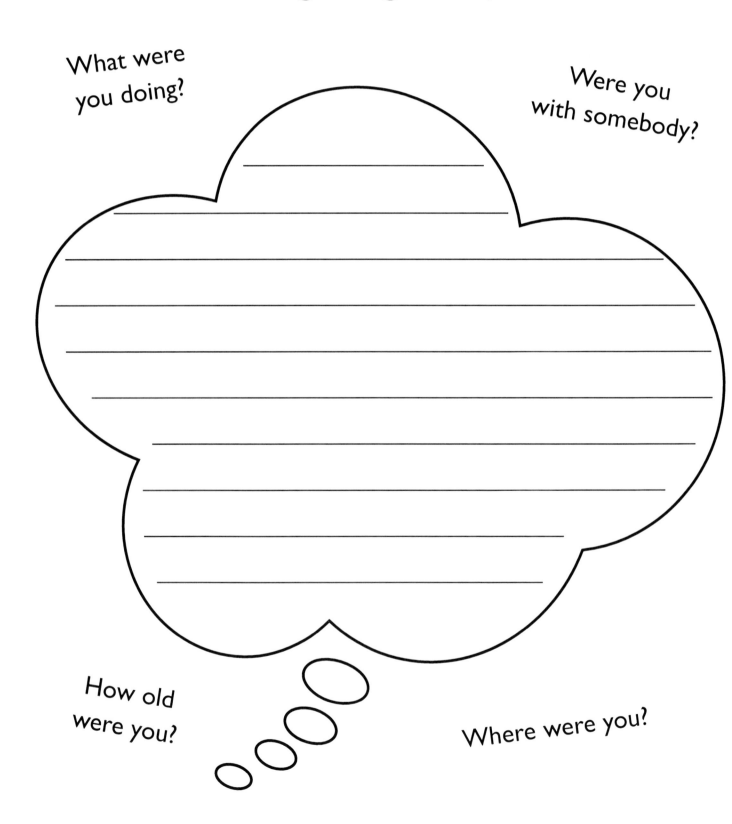

How old were you?

Where were you?

Draw a picture of your memory!

Here are some things you can do to Honor and Remember your pet...

Keep something that belonged to your pet
like a collar or a favorite toy.

Have a memorial service for your pet. Invite family and friends, and
everyone can think of something nice to say about your pet.

Plant some flowers or make a garden
and dedicate it to your pet.

Talk to people about your feelings and
how they're changing since your pet died.

Find a special place where you can
spend time thinking about or talking to your pet
(even though your pet is not here anymore).

Watch movies or look at
pictures of your pet.

Write thoughts about your pet
in a journal or diary.

Tie a message to a helium balloon or
think a special thought and let the balloon
go high into the sky.

Tie a
Note

Think a
Special
Thought

Remember all the good times you had with your pet
and how wonderful you felt when you were with your pet.

Can you think of other special ways
to remember your pet?

_____

_____

_____

_____

Use this activity book to remember your pet!

Look through this book or add to it whenever
you are thinking about and missing your pet.

Know that your pet will always be a part of
your life and who you are, and that it's OK to be
happy when you think about your pet.

Remember that as long as you have
loving thoughts about your pet,
he or she will live in your heart forever...
and will always be your FOREVER FRIEND.

Send us your drawings, poems, songs, stories, thoughts and letters!

Ask a grown-up to help you email: mystory@rainbowreach.com
or send snail mail to:
Rainbow Reach, 2340 Bedfordshire Circle, Reston, VA 20191

We'll add your materials to our website!*

Send a scan!

Send a photo of your work!

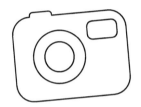 

Send original artwork!
If you would like original artwork returned, please include a self-addressed, stamped envelope.

Include as much (or as little) information as you like ... name (full name or first name only), age, and what your story is about.

Show and tell us how you are dealing with your difficult situation and we will share it to help other children.

Free Drawing Page

Use these extra pages to draw pictures or write your thoughts and feelings.
Fill them in now, or use them later when you are thinking about your pet.

Free Journal Page

_____

_____

_____

_____

_____

_____

_____

_____

_____

_____

_____

_____

_____

_____

_____

Free Drawing Page

Free Journal Page

_____

_____

_____

_____

_____

_____

_____

_____

_____

_____

_____

_____

_____

_____

_____

_____

_____

_____

Free Drawing Page

Free Journal Page

Free Drawing Page

Free Journal Page

Free Drawing Page

Free Journal Page

CPSIA information can be obtained at www.ICGtesting.com
Printed in the USA
BVOW050044170912

300399BV00010B/1/P